PRACTICAL COACHING SERIES

EMOTIONAL HACKING

Unleashing the Hidden Powers of Emotional Intelligence to Achieve More in Your Professional and Personal Life

BY ERIC DAVENPORT

Table of Contents

Introduction

*"Our emotions have a mind of their own,
one which can hold views quite
independently of our rational mind." –
Daniel Goleman*

Think of the last time you felt truly angry. Not just a little annoyed, but utterly enraged. What was it like? Perhaps it was empowering, energizing, and resulted in rational decisions that made your life a whole lot better – or not! Chances are that, in the heat of the moment, you did or said something you later regretted.

Whether or not they care to admit it, most people allow themselves to become consumed by their emotions at some point. Whether we feel too self-conscious to meet up with friends, too distracted by a breakup to get on with our work, or too furious to hold a calm conversation with our parents, there's no doubt that our feelings have consequences. To be more specific, our capacity to understand and express our emotions in a healthy way makes all the difference to our quality of life, the quality of our relationships, and even our career success. Handling our emotions – and those of other people – takes a special kind of skill. Unfortunately, this ability is overlooked in school. Instead, our parents and teachers are more interested in helping us pass exams and memorizing facts and figures. Most of us are familiar with the concept of intelligence, more commonly known as IQ. We often talk about "smart people" who make solving advanced equations, writing a novel, or completing a crossword look easy. These people tend to do well at school. They inspire envy in others.

To achieve an above-average score on a standard IQ test is a badge of honor in our society.

But does IQ equal success? If we go by popular wisdom, the answer is a resounding "Yes!" On an intuitive level, it makes sense that smart people should do well, right? But let's take a closer look at this assumption.

How many people do you know who achieved outstanding grades, yet never seemed to realize their full potential? We're all familiar with the stereotypical geek or the shy nerd – people who dazzle us with their intellectual brilliance, but never feel at ease in social situations or thrive in the workplace. You probably have at least one friend or relative who chronically underachieves. Everyone around them recognizes their IQ, but for some reason it never quite translates into all-round success.

What can we conclude from this? A high IQ might be a blessing, but it isn't enough. There's another secret ingredient that separates high-performing individuals from everyone else, and it isn't their academic prowess.

Introducing Emotional Intelligence

Emotional Intelligence, put in simple terms, is our mind's ability to perceive, understand, manage, and apply emotions effectively in real life. It is a relatively contemporary concept that was initially devised by Dr. John D. Mayer, Ph.D. and Dr. Peter Salovey, who said that Emotional Intelligence (or E.I.) is the ability to regulate our emotions and feelings and use them to guide our actions. Like I.Q., emotional Intelligence also varies from one person to another, and many of us remain unaware of how to spot and distinguish our emotional intellect or explore the power of the mind.

Getting fluent in the language of emotions can help us survive better in our relationships, at the workplace, and also have a healthy relationship with ourselves. Several studies over the years have shown that improving emotional intelligence can empower the mind and help us be more mindful and happy.

Are You Emotionally Intelligent?

Emotional Intelligence is the art of knowing where to hold yourself and where to let go, it is about finding your calm and knowing how to get the right balance between communication and silence.

Emotional intelligence, as manifested in real life is all about how well we can carry our feelings and express them in the right way. A well-balanced, empathetic, and sociable person is definitely more emotionally aware than an unempathetic and demotivated individual. The studies of Daniel Goleman, in his book on Emotional Intelligence published in 1995, illustrated the primary characteristics that are found in an emotionally intelligent person. An emotionally intelligent person is one who has:

- The ability to recognize one's own emotions
- The ability to relate to others' emotions
- The ability to listen to others without judging them
- The ability to actively participate in interpersonal communication and understand the nonverbal cues of behavior
- The ability to control one's thoughts and feelings
- The ability to effectively manage emotions and express them in a socially acceptable way

- The ability to receive criticisms positively and be able to benefit from them
- The power to forgive, forget, and move on rationally

How many of the above qualities can you relate yourself to?

If you have more than 5 of the above qualities, then it is an indicator that you have above average Emotional Intelligence. It is however a rare situation that all of the above qualities are demonstrated by one individual. That is why learning how to improve one's Emotional Intelligence is a continuous process.

E.Q. and I.Q.

"Emotional Intelligence is the ability to create a balance between knowing what you don't know and what you do know can be improved" – Proverb

The term "Emotional Intelligence" was first published in a paper by Michael Beldoch in 1964, but became popular in Daniel Goleman's 1995 book "Emotional Intelligence - Why it can matter more than IQ". Since then extensive research has been conducted in this field and several models are now being used on Emotional Intelligence, out of which the trait model, mixed model, and ability model are the well-known ones.

Intelligence was previously measured on the scale of I.Q. The higher a person's I.Q., the more intelligent would he/she be considered. To put it in simple words, I.Q. is how sharp you are to analyze and understand things logically, and E.Q. is the measure of how sharp you are to adapt to reality and survive in harmony with others around you. Emotional Quotient, or E.Q. is much more difficult to measure than a person's overall intelligence level. A high I.Q. does not guarantee a high E.Q. as well. A person having an I.Q. of above 100 (which is above the average level of intelligence) may have an E.Q. below average. Both the E.Q. and I.Q. are important in order to measure a person's overall intellectual ability. While the I.Q. will help in understanding his reasoning and problem-solving ability, the E.Q. will help in analyzing his empathy, emotional awareness, and sensitivity level.

Comparative Table

	Emotional Quotient	**Intelligence Quotient**
Abilities	Empathy, good interpersonal relationships, survival skills, ability to control impulses, thoughtful, sensitive	Logical, analytical mind, reasoning abilities, abstract thinking, problem solving abilities
Suitable professions	Team works and managerial responsibilities, individual business, social works, working with non-profit organizations for humanitarian causes, counseling, human resource jobs	Mathematical jobs, software and web development, linguistics, programming jobs

Tests that measure it	- Mayer-Salovey-Caruso Test - Daniel Goleman Model Test	- Stanford-Binet Intelligence Scale - Wechsler Intelligence Scale For Adults and Children

Chapter 1. Aspects of E.I. - Things We Need to Know

Before embarking on how to use Emotional Intelligence to our daily lives, let us first dive into some of the essential aspects of it.

How intelligently we use our emotions and feelings depends on four factors, as identified by Mayer and Salovey. According to them, the more we can work on improving these four areas, the happier can we be. They argued that an emotionally aware person is much better in interpersonal communication and sociability than someone who is unaware of his/her emotions and feelings.

The Four-Dimensional/ Four-Branch Model of Emotional Intelligence

Recognition: Who am I	**Self-Awareness**	**Social Awareness**
Regulation: What I do	**Self-Management**	**Social Skills**

The Four-Branch Model of E.I. was devised by Salovey and Mayer, 1990. It is an ability based model of emotional intelligence and it defines E.I. as the ability to express, integrate, and regulate emotions in a positive way. This model identifies four branches or dimensions of emotional intelligence:

1. **Perceiving Emotions** - How well a person can sense and interpret his emotions sets the mark for how emotionally intelligent he is likely to be. Perceiving emotions is the ability to identify how you feel and also the power to decipher what others feel from their expressions and words.

2. **Utilizing Emotions** - Emotions are extremely powerful. They guide our cognition and actions. An emotionally intelligent person can optimize his emotions and gain the most from it. They use their emotions in a way that can guide their actions and behavior positively.

3. **Comprehending Emotions** - The root of managing and utilizing emotions is the ability to understand them. Whether it is your own emotions or the feelings of someone else, the better a person is able to decode the language of emotions, the more emotionally aware will he/she become. Emotional intelligence is about being sensitive to what we feel and what we think others feel. With the component of empathy entwined with it, an emotionally intelligent person is able to identify and label our feelings.

4. **Regulating Emotions** - Regulating or managing emotions is the capacity to manage feelings in both ourselves and in others. Consequently, the emotionally intelligent individual can saddle feelings, even negative

ones, and oversee them to accomplish proposed objectives.

Chapter 2. Measuring Emotional Intelligence

Over the years, several measures of emotional intelligence have been developed by eminent researchers in this field. Most of these tests are self-administered, which means that they can be conducted without any expert supervision, and others are more structured ones that need to be administered by a professional clinician.

Why Should I Measure My Emotions?

Emotions are subjective and personal experiences that are never the same for two people. Unlike the I.Q. tests that have clearly classified people into different categories of intellectual levels based on their scores, it is difficult to get a similar frame when we are measuring our emotional intelligence and awareness. You may be wondering that if emotions are individualized, what is the whole point in measuring them? Why can't we just go and ask people how they feel and get an understanding of their emotional awareness? Here is why.

Emotional intelligence has a lot to do with the social, interpersonal and intrapersonal skills that we have. For example, a high achiever at work is not so just because of his professional skills. It is also because of his stress management abilities, communication skills, team performance and maybe leadership skills. All these abilities add up to make someone emotionally intelligent, and this is what is estimated in an Emotional Awareness/Intelligence Test.

How Can an Emotional Intelligence Test Help Me?

Testing your Emotional Intelligence is an important beginning in understanding where can one begin to improve it. These tests help us to:

- Evaluate the different aspects of our emotions
- Suggest ways to improve emotional awareness
- It provides information on our existing skills
- It helps us in improving our interpersonal relationships at the professional and personal level by giving a personal evaluation of which areas we should try to improve
- It allows us to realize to what extent do we know ourselves and also lets us explore the dimensions of the self we were not aware of
- It helps us in understanding emotions of ourselves as well as others, as a result making it easier to manage and regulate our expressions in socially acceptable ways.

Self-Report Emotional Intelligence Scale

The below test is a simple, yet effective way to understand where one stands in the ladder of Emotional Intelligence. All you will need is a pen, paper, and honesty to yourself while recording responses.

Instructions: Below are a set of 15 statements that describe you in different situations. Each statement has 5 options, where '1' stands for *not at all*, '2' stands for *rarely*, '3' stands for *occasionally*, '4' stands for *often*, and '5' stands for *very often*. Choose the option that you think is most suitable for you. After you have finished responding, calculate the total score and interpret your result following the norms provided below.

Statement	1 Not at all	2 Rarely	3 Occasionally	4 Often	5 Very often
1) I lose my temper very easily					
2) I can relate to others' emotions					
3) People say I am a great listener					
4) I find it hard to express my emotions					
5) I can adjust with my teammates at work					
6) I can get over something easily					
7) I feel upset when someone criticizes me					

(continued)

Statement	1 Not at all	2 Rarely	3 Occasionally	4 Often	5 Very often
8) I am well aware of what I am good and bad at					
9) I avoid communicating with people to avoid conflicts					
10) I enjoy organizing and managing events at work and home					
11) I can control my anger no matter what					
12) My heart cries out for all the homeless people out there					
13) I do not have frequent mood swings					
14) It is easy for me to initiate a conversation					
15) My friends can trust me with					

anything they want					

Score	Basic Interpretation of Results
1-25	You need to work a lot on building your emotional intelligence and awareness.
26-50	You have average emotional intelligence. A little bit of effort can do wonders for you. You may have a good interpersonal relationship at home or work, but you need to focus more on improving them and avoiding conflicts.
51-75	You are high on your emotional intelligence level. You are an active listener with an empathetic attitude. You can relate to others' emotions and you are working just fine with your personal and professional relationships.

Detailed Interpretation of Results

- If your score lies in the first category (**1-25**), it means that your E.Q. is below average. You need to work on building emotional awareness and improving your existing skills. There are several tips and self-help activities given in this book that will guide you through the process of becoming more emotionally aware. Keep reading.

- If your score lies in the second category (**26-50**), it means that you are average on E.I., but you still need to work on improving it. People who lie under this category may be able to express emotions positively but lag behind in empathy, or vice versa. It implies that they have not fully mastered over all the aspects of emotional intelligence yet. Some might be great managers at the office but poor husbands at home, some may be great as a teacher but de-motivating as a father. You will find many activities with examples in the following chapters that will open your perspective and allow you to become high on your E.I.

- If your score lies in the third category (**51-75**), it means that you have high emotional intelligence. You are able to empathize with others, understand them, express your emotions and manage them positively. That challenge for you is to maintain this virtue in all walks of life - be that as a professional, a spouse, or a parent. And this is why you need to focus on being aware of your own thoughts and feelings.

Other Standard Tests of Emotional Intelligence

The below list is compiled for optional self-learning purpose, in case you decide to invest more time into learning about yourself, using various alternative models of Emotional Intelligence measurement.

Mayer-Salovey-Caruso EI Test (MSCEIT)

The Mayer-Salovey-Caruso Test for Emotional Intelligence was developed and based on the EI model of Emotional Intelligence by Mayer and Salovey. It measures the four dimensions of the Mayer-Salovey model

- Perception

- Facilitation

- Understanding

- Management of emotions.

The MSCEIT consists of 141 items and provides 15 main and 3 supplement scores.
Link to the detailed test description:
www.eiconsortium.org/measures/msceit.html

Emotional Quotient Inventory (EQI)

Daniel Goleman had developed an easy and interesting way of measuring how well a person is in control of his/her emotions. It is a quiz called the Emotional Quotient Inventory or the BarOn Emotional Intelligence Test. It is a self-report measure organized in a structured manner with close-ended questions. The scale measures a person's emotional awareness in the fields of:

- Self-perception

- Interpersonal relationships

- Decision-making

- Self-perception

- Stress management

The test is available in multiple versions and is generally recommended for individuals above the age of 18.

Link to the detailed test description:

http://www.eiconsortium.org/measures/eqi.html

Genos Emotional Intelligence Scale (GEIS)

The Genos Scale for Emotional Intelligence is a specifically designed test for measuring emotional intelligence and awareness of people at work. It measures their behavior in the workplace and is an indicator of how well a person can perform and achieve at work. The key areas that the Genos Test for Emotional Intelligence measure are:

- Emotional Self-Awareness

- Emotional Expression

- Interpersonal Emotional Awareness

- Interpersonal Emotional Management

- Emotional Reasoning

- Self-Management

- Self-Control

The test is generally conducted under the supervision of a skilled professional. It is widely used by Human Resource Professionals and Counselors operating in corporate or other professional areas, to gain a good understanding of the nature and emotional stability of the employees. It consists of 70 items and takes a short time for administration.

Link to the detailed test description:

www.eiconsortium.org/measures/genos.html

Wong's Scale of Emotional Intelligence (WEIS)

The Wong's Scale of Emotional Intelligence was developed by Wong et. al in 2007 and measures emotional awareness of the respondent in two parts. It is a self-report measure and is also based on the four dimensions of the El Model of Emotional Intelligence. The first part of the WEIS is a situational test consisting of 20 scenarios. The respondents here are required to choose the scenario that best describes them. The second part of the test is an ability test where respondents are given 20 ability pairs. The respondents at this stage are required to choose one out of the two options in each pair that best reflect their strengths and awareness.

Link to the detailed test description:

www.eiconsortium.org/measures/weis.html

The Practical Guide to Emotional Intelligence

Chapter 3. Emotional Intelligence at Work

"CEOs are hired for their intellect and business expertise - and fired for a lack of emotional intelligence." – Daniel Goleman

According to a survey by Career Builders in 2011, which was conducted on hiring managers, it was found that 71% of them preferred selecting employees on the basis of how emotionally intelligent they were, rather than estimating just their I.Q. The value of emotional intelligence is well perceived in the professional and personal spheres of life. Especially at the workplace, emotional intelligence helps in:

- Communicating effectively with colleagues, superiors, and subordinates

- Performing well in group activities and maintaining a high team spirit throughout

- Organizing and managing daily work schedules

- Sustaining motivation in work and facing criticisms positively

- Becoming a good leader

Many psychologists and mental health professionals believe that emotional intelligence is an important aspect in achieving success at work. Employees who are emotionally intelligent and aware, have a better interpersonal relationship with their supervisors and are able to maintain their work-life balance better than others.

An organization that is emotionally intelligent has employees who are:

- Self-motivated
- Productive
- Committed to their professions
- Confident and dynamic in nature
- Empathetic and socially communicative
- Well-rewarded
- Self-aware and self-controlled

Leading with Emotional Intelligence

Leaders with high emotional intelligence are likely to make the most of their efforts and have a positive impact on people they are supervising. Many organizations have specially trained programs conducted by professionals that help in educating employees about emotional intelligence, assessing their E.Q. levels and training them to improve their E.I.

Signs of a leader with high E.I.

A person with high E.Q. is likely to manifest the following behavioral patterns:

- Give positive feedback and appreciate workers for giving results
- Accept his/her responsibility for anything that goes wrong in the group
- Never playing the blame game or the role of a victim
- Expressing anger in a way that others won't feel bad or insulted
- Integrating and actively communicating with the team as often as needed
- Being open to others' opinions and criticisms

In specific situations, representatives with high emotional insight are better ready to participate and communicate with others, oversee business related pressure, settle clashes that may emerge inside working environment connections, and gain from past relational mistakes. Though emotional awareness may not be the fundamental requirement for each job, it can be a key quality for the vast majority in administration and leading positions. To be powerful pioneers in the work environment, chiefs, bosses, one must have the capacity to work profitably with individuals under their charge. A decent leader can make the sort of workplace where every individual feels important and roused to succeed.

Tips to Improve Leadership Skills with Emotional Intelligence

Pioneers with high E.Q. can utilize their social aptitudes to cultivate affinity and trust with people they work with. They tend to see their colleagues as people with abilities, foundations, and identities. Like every other connection, work connections may encounter issues at some point or another. At the point when a conflict emerges, supervisors with high E.I. are able to control their intrinsic motivation, see the circumstance from all viewpoints, and look for commonly gainful arrangements.

If you are working in a leading or managerial position and aim to improve your skills at work, here are some tips for you:

- Assess your emotional intelligence once or twice a year and maintain the records
- Keep a close eye on how you communicate with your subordinates and seniors. If you are emotionally aware, you will be able to self-analyze where your communication is going wrong
- Call for regular stand up meetings where you can discuss and gain insight on the work progress
- Encourage your teammates to communicate more with each other and come to you if they are facing any difficulty
- Allow your teammates to openly voice their opinions. Encourage feedback and face criticisms with a positive mind
- Always maintain a good working rapport with your clients as well as colleagues. Communicate with them if there arises even the slightest hitch and work for resolving the issue
- Work hard, but take frequent intervals as well. Try not to work for more than 9 hours a day and take sufficient rest.

Professional Networking with Emotional Intelligence

"It is very important to understand that emotional intelligence is not the opposite of intelligence, it is not the triumph of heart over the head - it is the unique intersection of both." – David Caruso

---

So why are we talking about professional networking and emotional intelligence in the same breath? Of course, they don't sound quite intertwined, but let me tell you, they are. Why do we need business networking at all? I am sure your answer lies somewhere here:

- Making new connections Improving business liaison
- Reaching targets and deadlines
- Making more profit
- Keeping clients engaged and maintaining their trust.

And for all of these things to be accomplished successfully, we need to be aware of what we say and how we present our thoughts. We can afford to sound stupid once in a while at home, but we just cannot afford anything less than perfection in our professional fields. That is where we need to perform our best every day, and it can be really stressful at times.

How Emotions Hijack Networking

This is a picture of what happens when two people are engaged in communication:

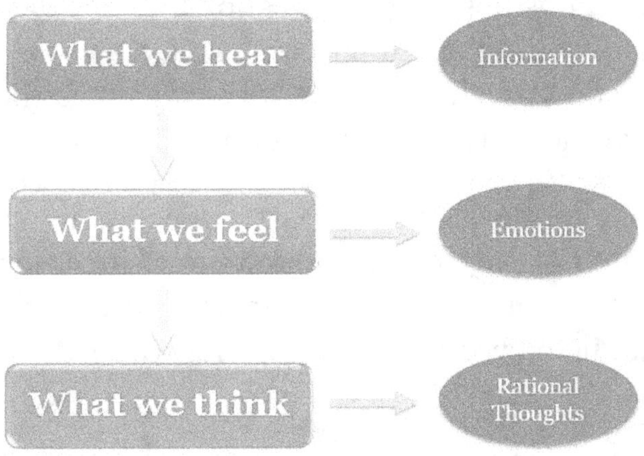

For some people, business networking is a piece of cake, but for some, it is not. Some of us find it really difficult to keep the balance between what we feel, what we think, and how we express it. However, people who are emotionally intelligent and aware can easily get through this as they have:

- **Self-Confidence** - Emotionally intelligent people have it just right. They neither sound too proud nor too intimidated. With too high confidence, you may sound proud and disregardful of others. On the other hand, too little self-confidence will hold you back from expressing your thoughts rationally. Tips on how to get the balance and make long-lasting business networks are mentioned below.

- **Positivity** - The ability to put your thoughts to the world in the most acceptable manner. High E.I. people are able to control their flow of emotions when they are in that professional setting and avoid conflicts effectively.

- **Empathy** - The willingness to identify and recognize the feelings of others and internalizing them as your own. Emotionally intelligent people are better networkers as they use empathy as the magic ingredient in all business communications. It not only makes the conversation more successful, it also makes the other person gain full trust in you. And it is this trust that takes networking to the next level.

Coming to the practical part, some of us can be great workers but not-so-great networkers. And it is only natural, we can't be an all-rounder all the time. Here are some tips for you that can help you with your networking skills in the professional field.

Tips to Improve Emotional Intelligence in Professional Networking

Listen before you say

A great quality of good networkers is the ability to listen actively and be empathetic. People who have a high E.I. are able to listen, understand, and act in a way that suits both parties. Besides giving you a strong business accomplice, it will also let the other person gain full trust in you.

Come straight to the point

If you are a part of a professional discussion, it is always good to be straightforward. Talk about the scheduled dates and time frame openly to avoid any hitch later. Make sure to have all the terms and conditions settled before you dive into the work. There is no need to make business communications flowery as long as you stand true to your point.

Be informative

When you are talking with your business associates, make sure that you sound informative. Even if you feel anxious, use your rational thinking to gather all the information in your head and express it as coherently as you can. Being Emotionally Intelligent will help you gaining grip over the unreasonable anxieties that can damage your performance.

Use your big-name stamps

A clever tactic of getting the hang of it, is by mentioning about your past success, subtly. Knowing about your previous accomplishments may help the clients in gaining more trust on your work and at the same time, it will also make the network much stronger.

Have a clear plan

Make a blueprint and a to-do list before any important work. Not that it will make you emotionally intelligent, but will definitely make you gain a clear vision and you will know which areas need more focus. Most successful leaders are successful because of the planned and structured way that they incorporate in work.

Moving Up the Ladder - Success and E.I.

> *"Emotional Intelligence, more than any other factor, more than I.Q. or expertise, accounts for 85% to 90% success at work... I.Q. is a threshold competence. You need it, but it doesn't make you a star. Emotional Intelligence can."* – Warren Bennis

Is Emotional Intelligence a predictor of success? Or does it work the other way?

There is no certain evidence yet that E.I. guarantees success or vice versa. However, extensive research backed by scientific evidence has proved the fact that people who are emotionally intelligent and more aware, can achieve and handle success better than others who are not.

All these discussions on E.I. boil down to the question how we can move up the success ladder using our emotional intelligence. Daniel Goleman in one of his research had mentioned that *"I.Q. is a better predictor of what work is more suitable for you, but once you have got placed in that profession, you are competing with other people who are just as intelligent and educated as you"*. This is where E.I. comes into the picture. While I.Q. helps you decide what is best suited for you, E.I. helps you to survive in that profession by regulating your thoughts, feelings, and behavior in the professional setup.

Successful leaders and entrepreneurs do believe that it is their rational thinking, awareness, and the ability to communicate effectively, that has helped them a lot in getting them where they wanted to go. In the following section, we have a list of some self-help activities which can help you improve your E.I. at work and have a positive impact on your overall professional success as a whole. Let's keep reading.

Self-Help Activities for Improving E.I. at Work

My Weekly Planner

Improving E.I. at work is a continuous process. Planning and scheduling your days in an organized way is a good start to decluttering your mind. Keep a weekly planner where you can jot down your tasks for the week priority wise. Whenever your mind goes astray, you can have a look at your tasks and bring it back to focus.

Thought Journal

Get into the habit of keeping a diary where you can note down the thoughts that are ruling your mind at the moment. For example, if you got bullied at the office today, write down how you felt about it. Note down all the positive and negative thoughts that come to your mind. Thought journaling helps you to objectify your own feelings and get a better hold at managing them.

Go for people watching

A large part of E.I. includes understanding and relating to others, especially if you are the owner, leader or a supervisor. But often we are so engrossed in our own worlds that we fail to notice what is going on around us. Go out of your cabin for 10 minutes every day, take a walk around your office, have small talks with your colleagues and subordinates, observe how they are interacting with each other and feel the ambiance of your office overall. This is a great way to improve awareness and learn more about people you work with.

Count to 10 before you react

When under a stressful situation where you find it hard to hold yourself back from reacting, count backward from 10 to 1 very slowly. If possible, repeat it twice followed by two deep breaths. Allow yourself to do this every time before you lash out. You will see that the pressure of bursting out your emotions has subsided and now you can talk about it in a fruitful manner.

E.I. Assessment

It is also a good idea to keep a check on your E.I. level once or twice a year. The results will keep you in perspective and let you know when you need to start working on it. You can take professional help for this, or just try with a test which we presented for you earlier in this book.

Chapter 4. Emotional Intelligence and Relationships

Relationships can cause dramatic swings in emotions. Whether it is marriage, parenthood, or the love for your own parents, there is always a heavy flow of emotions in relationships. People go from loving someone to the moon and back, and then they can suddenly start hating the same person when life kicks its way in. Each emotion that is associated with our loved ones - be that love, anger, jealousy, or hatred, is powerful; so powerful that it can take up all our headspace making our mind totally cluttered and confused. And whatsoever, you might end up lashing out at your kid or asking for a divorce from your partner, because you feel mentally exhausted.

Emotional Intelligence is the most important factor for making a relationship successful. And this is because emotion is the root of any human relationship. To learn how to express yourself and manage your emotions in the most intelligent way is the key to have a successful relationship. In this section, we will have a look at the various areas of interpersonal relationships and how emotional intelligence can make a real difference. Keep reading to know more about it.

The Basics

Dr. Athena Staik, a specialist in this field has recognized the importance of being emotionally aware of a love or a marital relationship. Her studies have revealed that emotionally intelligent couples are more mindful towards their actions and thoughts. They can handle conflicts and are able to focus on the solutions rather than problems.

Consider the following situations.

Situation #1

You had an ugly fight with your partner and you are just on the verge of giving up. You feel there is nothing left to be discussed and it won't change anything about him/her. You keep on brooding over the same thought day and night until the time comes when you feel emotionally drained.

Situation #2

You had an ugly fight with your partner and you both have stopped talking to each other. You are fed up and feel that your relationship is hanging on the cliff. You start thinking, and instead of ruminating over the bad memories, you take a minute to recollect all the beautiful memories that you have had together.

Which of the above reactions do you think an emotionally intelligent person would have?

If you just thought "Situation 2", you are absolutely right. An emotionally intelligent person would always focus on solving the problem and building a long-lasting relationship. He/she would keep an even balance of the good things and bad things before jumping to any conclusion.

Emotional Intelligence in a relationship is all about developing the three magic skills:

- **Empathy** - The ability to walk in others' shoes and see the world from their perspective.

- **Respect** - The ability to regard others for what they have done and acknowledge their abilities, keeping aside personal views. At the same time, it is also equally important to have regard and respect for oneself and being aware of the self-worth.
- **Expression** - The ability to let others know what we feel, but in a socially acceptable way.

Is My Partner Emotionally Intelligent?

A great deal of discomfort arises in relationships when one partner is ready to give it all but the other is not ready to acknowledge it. We must remember that to keep a relationship flowing smooth, both the partners must be emotionally aware of each other. They must be able to give out the emotions that they want to receive, and manage their feelings in a prudent way. But having said so, it is also impractical to go for an E.Q. test every time you get into a relationship. However, if you want to gain an insight into your partner's emotional awareness, here are some quick tips that might be helpful.

Your partner is emotionally intelligent if he/she:

- Is able to express his/her feelings positively
- Remembers the small things that can affect you and the relationship - both positively and negatively
- Is ready to talk it out whenever things start falling out of place
- Is focused on taking the relationship to the next stage rather than fighting over petty matters
- Shares household chores and responsibilities
- Praises your efforts instead of nagging all the time

- Can read your expressions and body language

- Understands your situation and is ready to make adjustments for keeping the relationship going.

Tips to Improve E.I. in Relationships

If you find your spouse or partner lacking these qualities, consider on taking some measures on improving their E.I. skills. Here are some tips that can help you in improving emotional intelligence in your relationships and make them long-lasting.

Devote time

I miss our years of courtship. We hardly go out now.

Don't let this be you. Spend time with your partner. Go on drives, cook together, eat out, sing aloud, do whatever makes you both happy. The more time you devote to your relationship, the better will you be able to reflect each other's emotions.

Understand the NVCs

I don't know what is wrong with my wife. She is not even looking at me today.

You become truly aware of your partner's emotions if you are able to understand them without their saying so. Notice what your partner tries to convey through his/her body language and NVC (Nonverbal Communication) Cues. For example, if he/she is not making eye contact while talking, or is not kissing you back as he/she usually does, it is time for you to ask if something is wrong.

Do not avoid the rough talks

I heard my husband talking over the phone about moving out. Is he planning to change his job? But what about me and our kids?

Keeping secrets is not allowed in any relationships. It just leads the way to unnecessary doubts and eventually kills the love. Never step back from initiating conversations with your partner, no matter how awkward it may be. Whether it is about your ex, or your career, or your parents moving in with you, talk it out. The true sign of emotional intelligence lies in resolving conflicts and not bottling them up.

Criticize, but don't hurt

Maylie takes 2 hours in bathroom every day, and I get late for her. This is so annoying!

Accept the fact that nobody is perfect, neither you nor your partner. There have to be some things you don't like about each other. Tell your partner and discuss the things that can be sorted. Adjust where you can and let your partner know where you are finding it difficult. But make sure that you don't express in a way that it hurts him/her, or make him/her feel less important. And especially, never criticize your partner in public.

Focus on solutions

David has been spending all his money and not saving anything for our future.

No relationship is always perfect and rosy. When life kicks its way in, we have to make some important choices that would reframe our lives. But whatever be the situation and no matter how serious conflicts may arise, set aside some time where you both can talk to each other and find a way out. Become aware of what you and your partner are feeling and focus on building the relationship. It takes a second to break someone's heart, but if you are emotionally intelligent, you will know what to do to make the relationship last forever. We must remember that *"Tough times never last, but tough people do."*

Be there

My partner just lost his job. He is heartbroken and I am scared it might affect our relationship.

The biggest thing that you can give your partner is being there when he/she needs you the most. Do not try to judge your partner if you cannot feel what he/she is going through. Just stay by their side and keep encouraging them. This works great if you really want to improve your emotional awareness in the relationship.

Self-Help Activity to Improve Emotional Intelligence in Relationships

Exercise 1 - Thought Listing

Take some time out every month where you and your partner can practice this exercise. It is simple. Take a white sheet of blank paper and a pen, and give one to your partner. On one side of the paper write down all the negative thoughts and things that you hate about your partner. After you are done, turn the page and start jotting down all the good things and fond memories that you two have shared with each other. After you finish writing, exchange the list with each other and read both the sides silently. What do you feel? Are the fights and misunderstandings worth spoiling all those beautiful memories? Or is it worth keep trying to save your relationship with the one who means so much?

Exercise 2 - Mind Watching Device

We often do not consider improving our E.I. unless there arises a need. However, psychologists have approved the fact that keeping an eye on our E.I. on a daily basis helps us in becoming more aware and reduces the probability of sudden emotional breakdowns. A great advancement in this field is the mind watching devices that help in monitoring our own thoughts and emotions and gaining knowledge on what to improve. There are devices like the Mind Watch and the Emotive that are able to record our thoughts and feelings through advanced EEG and brain imaging systems. They let us know when our thoughts are going astray and make us more aware of our own minds. Not just for emotional intelligence in relationships, having a mind watch is recommended for improving the overall emotional intelligence level on every aspect of life.

Exercise 3 - Critical Dates

This may sound strange, but it's worth a try. Arrange a critical date with your partner once or twice a month. Book for dinner or just go for a walk, just the two of you, where you talk and discuss only the things that are not going right in your relationship. Talk openly about all the bad habits, the late night returns, the failed promises, and everything that you had been bottling up so far. But remember -

- You cannot shout
- You cannot leave before the date is over
- You cannot judge
- You will let your partner speak
- You will express whatever you feel without any hesitation

After having such open conversations, you can see how relieved you feel and both of you will get to know each other better than you did.

Chapter 5. Emotional Intelligence and Parenthood

When talking about E.I. and parenthood, I have seen most discussions focusing on how parents can train their kids to be more emotionally aware. But here's the truth - if you are not emotionally aware as a parent, you cannot expect your child to show the same thing. Children are great imitators, and the best way they learn something is by observing it around them. Hence, the skills of emotional intelligence are learned by children when they see adults around them showing the same behaviors.

So what does it mean to be an emotionally intelligent parent?

Scientific research and studies over the years have revealed that children who are raised by emotionally intelligent parents are mentally and physically healthier, better adjusted socially, high academic achievers, and have stronger parent-child bonding.

Emotionally intelligent parents are those who:

- Foster positivity in the child

- Focus on reducing stress and complexity

- Encourages the child to be more creative and resilient

- Nourish their children with compassion and peace of mind

- Help their children grow as a positive change-maker

Tips to Improve E.I. as a Parent

Be a part of your child's everyday life

I doubt if my dad knows which standard I am in.
The first step in improving your emotional awareness as a parent is to become more and more involved in your child's daily life. Participate in his daily duties like doing homework or packing for school. Have simple conversations like "How was your day?" or "What are you planning to do next?" Talk to their teachers and counselors to know how they are performing and where they are lagging behind. These small things will make you much more emotionally intelligent towards your relationship with your child.

Manage your relationships

My parents are always fighting at home. I hate to be a part of it.
The key to a healthy parent-child relationship is a healthy marriage. If you cannot handle your relationship with your partner, you are bound to lose focus on your children. Avoid bringing your marital conflicts in front of your kids, and in any case, if you do so, make sure you resolve them in front your children as well.

Talk, talk, and talk

My mom is my best friend. I can tell her about anything that is going on in my life.

If your child can say this from the core of his/her heart, know that you are a successful and an emotionally intelligent parent. It has been proven that active communication between parents and children allow them to know and empathize with each other. Even if your kid is still an infant, spend some time talking with him/her. The emotional exchange that happens through one-on-one communications lays the foundation for positive parenting.

Listen, don't judge

I was caught smoking with my friends and I don't know how to tell my parents about it.

Parenting can be a really difficult task at times, especially when kids reach puberty. To be a positive and aware parent, you must be able to accept your child with all his/her positive and negative sides. Be an active listener; give your child space so that he/she can come up to you with their problems and feel safe to share them with you. Avoid being judgmental, instead focus on guiding him/her to do the right things. Even if you are angry, train your mind to express it in a way that wouldn't make your child feel bad. If as a parent you can master your emotions, you will surely be successful in raising a high E.Q. child as well.

Explain the rules, don't inflict them

If you want your child to learn something, explain why they should learn it and what will happen if they don't. For example, if you are telling your child not to spank street dogs, tell him/her that it will hurt them and ask them how they would have felt if somebody did the same thing to them. Pressurizing a child to follow rules may give immediate results, but it does not make him/her internalize the positive behavior.

As the famous saying goes, *parents don't make children, children make parents* - so is true. Parenting is a long journey that keeps changing its shape and style. Not only does a child grows from an infant to an adult, parents also grow with them, and being emotionally intelligent makes this journey more meaningful and the most valuable asset that we have in our lives.

Self-Help Activity to Improve Emotional Intelligence in Parenting

Exercise 1 - Personal narrative

A renowned mental health professional Dan McAdams said that "the stories that we tell our kids don't just help children in shaping their personalities, it also helps them understand ours".

Spend time with your kids where you share your childhood memories with him/her. Not only will it comfort your child, it will also make you become aware of the fact that you were no different as a child. And the best part of it is that it brings you closer to your child.

Exercise 2 - Stress Release

Stress holds us back from expressing and managing our emotions positively. Especially for parents, who are struggling with so many issues every day, it is very important to keep some time aside where you can practice meditation and stress release. A few techniques are mentioned here:

- **Deep breathing** – Sit in a calm and isolated place and take two deep breaths at first. Then, close your eyes and start inhaling on a count of 3 and exhaling on a count of 5. Repeat this for 10-15 minutes and you will notice the difference.
- **Mindful Music Therapy** – Tune in to your favorite songs, preferably mild tunes. You can create a playlist beforehand or play as you like. Turn down the volume so that it is not harsh to the ears and dim the lights of the room you are in. Immerse yourself completely to

the tune and let your mind float with the melody. Allow your mind to wander for a while and forget about all the daily hassles of life. Practice this as often as you want to, for no less than a 15-20 minutes period. It is a wonderful stress release mechanism.

- **Muscle Relaxation** – Ease your muscles when you feel too stressed and start losing focus. Lie down on a comfortable bed or couch and focus on each muscle starting from head to toe. For relaxing them, clench the particular muscle and hold for a count of 10, and then release it slowly. By the time you finish relaxing all your muscles, you can feel the difference from when you had started.

- **Cheating on food** – No one should be blamed for this one! Allow yourself to gobble on all the delicious savories once or twice a week. Forget about the calorie count and the sugar levels, just eat whatever you feel like and eat until you are full. It will immediately fill your heart with joy and in the blink of an eye, you will feel de-stressed. But yes, do remember too much of any good thing is not good for us.

- **Do what you love** – Once in a while, do what you love doing. We all have that passion, that one thing that makes us forget all the woes of life - painting, playing the guitar, doing crafts, shopping, baking, that can be anything. Take some time out for yourself where you can pursue your passion, and you will see life isn't that bad as it seems to be.

Exercise 3 - Switching Roles

Being parents, we often lose insight on how we felt when we were kids. Playing role reversing is a way that can help parents gaining awareness and empathize with their kids.

Make up a situation, anything common like helping your child with his Maths homework. Take up the child's role and let the child be you for some time. Seeing how your kids are portraying you will make you aware of how you have presented yourself to them. Walking in the kid's shoe will also make you aware of how the child might be feeling when he makes a mistake and gets scolded by you. And in this whole process, what you gain is your emotional awareness towards your kid.

Chapter 6. Emotional Intelligence and Health

E.I. and the Body

"He who has health, has hope; and he who has hope, has everything." -- Arabian Proverb

---

Think of this.

You have been working for hours at stretch and skipped lunch. After some time, you start starving, you feel hungry like anything. What would you do?

I am sure you will just go and grab a good lunch, freshen up, and come back to work. And that is just the right thing to do. But what would have happened if you could not feel your hunger at the right time and go on working till you ran out of all your energy?

Hunger, in this example, is the emotion that you were feeling. Acknowledging it at the right time made you eat food and manage it. Had you not paid attention to it and taken the necessary steps to satiate yourself, it would have caused you physical trouble (for eg you could feel dizzy or have a headache), and eventually, you would lose focus from work.

Paying attention to emotions at the right time does not only help us in dealing with life situations positively, it also impacts on our physical and mental health. The Trait Meta-Mood Scale (TMMS), has shown that Emotional Intelligence significantly affects our physical health. The TMSS approach speaks of 3 core aspects of E.I., which is a little different from the four branch model we had discussed before. According to it, the 3 aspects of E.I. are:

- **Attention** - The ability to focus and pay heed to what we feel

- **Clarity** - The ability to understand our emotions

- **Maintenance** - The ability to maintain a positive mood and recover from negative emotions effectively.

This approach to E.I. made it easier for us to understand how emotional awareness can affect our body. Keep reading to know more about the ways your health is related to your Emotional Intelligence.

How Emotions Affect the Body

Studies have shown that emotional stress and dysregulation can affect the way in which our body functions. A person who is emotionally aware of himself/herself and his/her surroundings is more likely to be healthier and stress-free. Out of the several areas of physical functioning that emotions impact on, some of the important ones are mentioned below:

- Emotional functioning is directly related to our cardiovascular functions. People who stress more and do nothing about it, or indulge in negative thinking are more likely to suffer from hypertension and cardiac problems.

- Emotional regulation is closely associated with hormonal balance in the body and vice versa. Just like hormonal dysregulation, for example during pregnancy, makes a woman emotionally vulnerable, emotional unawareness, in general, can cause hormones fluctuate and cause health issues like ovarian cysts and fibroids.

- Emotions also affect our enzymatic and digestive functions. Prolonged stress and emotional turmoils reduce our normal digestive functioning and can cause symptoms like burning in the stomach, constipation, and indigestion.

In the upcoming section, we will explore the several ways emotions affect our body, mind, and overall well-being, and discuss some useful tips and tricks on improving E.I. to stay healthy.

E.I. and the Mind - Handling Stress with Emotional Intelligence

Mental Health and emotional intelligence go hand in hand. If you are aware of what you feel and are in control of the ways you express it, you are definitely in possession of a good mental health. The more you are in conflict with yourself or people around you, the more stressed you will feel, and eventually, lose your mental well-being.

To improve your emotional intelligence, you must continue to work on protecting your emotions and sharpen your self-awareness <u>every day</u>.

What can cause stress?

Stress is nothing but our body's natural way to respond to any change. Stress can be positive (Eustress) or negative (Distress), depending upon the emotions they evoke and the situations that trigger them. But normally it is the negative stress that we generally refer to while talking about stress management and emotional awareness. We all are capable of handling stress up to a certain limit, crossing which can make us feel emotionally overwhelmed and cause several physical and psychological hazards.

There are several situations that may evoke stress. Some of the more common ones are:

- Death of someone close

- Losing a job

- Infidelity

- Breakup or divorce

- Getting bullied at work or at home

- Increasing conflict in relationships

- Work hazards

- Financial crisis

- Getting diagnosed with a serious medical condition

- Exposure to traumatic events like natural disaster, accidents, rape, or public humiliation

Exposure to such stressful situations impairs the way we think. We become so overwhelmed with the sudden emotions that we lose focus and start thinking irrationally. You can know that you are stressed when you:

- Cannot concentrate on any work

- Have a general feeling of sadness and irritability

- Can see only the negative side of things

- Worry constantly about things that you cannot control

- Have a loss of appetite
- Have reduced sleep and loss of sex drive
- Prefer to stay alone and refrain from socializing
- Feel demotivated to work
- Don't want to see your friends or go out with them
- Have sudden emotional outbursts that you can't explain
- Have a fluctuating mood all day

If you are facing 5 or more of these symptoms for over a period of time, then it is a clear indication that you are under stress and losing your emotional awareness. To understand the relationship between stress and emotional intelligence, let us discuss a little about the associated neurological functions.

Brain Hijack

For any emotion that we feel, there are two areas of the brain responsible -

- **The Limbic System** - or the 'feeling' brain that makes us emotional and is responsible for making us happy, sad, or angry, and

- **The Prefrontal Cortex** - or the 'thinking' brain that helps us in thinking and rationalizing our emotions, such that we can express and manage them positively.

Stress reduces emotional awareness of ourselves and those around us, making us lose control over the way we think and feel, and all of that, in turn, increase the stress. And this cycle keeps repeating itself until we consciously take control of it.

While it is true that we cannot control our happiness or sadness in certain situations, we must also be aware of not getting too overwhelmed by it. Here are some tips that can help you in managing stress with emotional intelligence.

Tips to Manage Stress with Emotional Intelligence

Start with self-awareness

Self-Awareness is the first step towards emotional intelligence. If you devote some time to understanding what is going on in your mind and how your reactions can change the way you feel, you can become more emotionally intelligent. Keep an eye on the upcoming section on self-help activities where I have mentioned some great ways to improve self-awareness.

Handle one problem at a time

Job stress, sick parents, busy husband, kids who never stop crying - I so hate my life!

Does this sound familiar?

There are certain times when we have to deal with multiple life stressors. We may start feeling overburdened when we try to solve all problems at once and end up losing self-control. With the intense emotional turmoil and stress, we start reacting negatively. Instead of trying to be the jack of all, it is better if we try to be the master of one, in this case. What I mean is, try to handle each problem at a time, address the ones that are higher on your priority list and don't worry about the rest till you get off the first one. Take baby steps to manage each problem at a time. Break up your goals and try to achieve them one at a time. This can help you in reducing stress and remain emotionally aware at the same time.

Take out some me-time

This can be a very useful tip if you want to reduce your stress in an emotionally intelligent way. Take out some time for yourself every day, and spend this time only with yourself. Take a walk, go for a massage, have a coffee in your favorite place, or listen to some music. Spending some time pampering the self, help us to regain clarity and declutter the mind. It allows you to question yourself and look for answers that lie within. Try this and observe how you can effectively change the way you react to stressors.

Talk when you can

One of the most important aspects of emotional intelligence, which is self-expression, is damaged when we are stressed. Especially during interpersonal conflicts, we may react in either of the negative ways:

- Bottle up what we feel and later burst like a volcano

- Show uncontrolled temper and get into a nasty fight with the other person.

To avoid either of this, communicate before it is too late. Talking about what is disturbing you may be awkward in the beginning, but avoiding will only make it worse.

Self-Help Exercises to Improve Health and Reduce
Stress with Emotional Intelligence

Exercise 1 - Quality Listing

You can also call it a self-judgment test. The basic idea of this test is to improve your emotional intelligence by making you more aware of yourself. On practicing this every once or twice a week, you will feel much more confident about yourself and the way you see people around you. It helps in widening your perspective and lets you manage stress with optimism. You can use a paper pen or follow this standard template.

<table>
<tr><td>

Quality Listing

1. Three words that describe you the best:
    A)
    B)
    C)

2. Three best adjectives that suits your mood:
    A)
    B)
    C)

3. Three people who loves you the most and why:
    A)
    B)
    C)

</td></tr>
</table>

4. Three people you love the most and why:
    A)
    B)
    C)

5. Three things that you want to achieve in your life:
    A)
    B)
    C)

6. Three things that make you feel proud about yourself:
    A)
    B)
    C)

7. Three things you feel you should change about yourself:
    A)
    B)
    C)

Exercise 2 - Mindful Everyday

Mindfulness is the art of being present in the now and here. It is the perfect way of embracing reality and accepting what 'is'. There are many exercises and training modules of mindfulness available everywhere nowadays, but to improve your emotional intelligence and stay healthy, the best mindfulness practice is using your sense organs carefully. Through vision, smell, touch, taste, and hearing, you can become more conscious of yourself and surroundings. Be fully aware of what you see, touch, taste, or feel. Come closer to yourself and listen to what your body is telling you. People who practice mindfulness as a daily habit and almost 50% more emotionally intelligent than others.

You can try this for example - Go out for a nature walk as often as you can. Feel the breeze touching you gently, smell the fresh air, and behold the beauty of everything that you see. See how you feel alive and rejuvenated instantly.

Exercise 3 - Mood Mapping

Our mood is the natural indicator of emotions. How our mood fluctuates can tell us how well or how bad we are able to manage our emotions. Mood mapping is a well-known technique to monitor your emotions. All you need to do is chart out how you feel once or twice a week, trace out what made you feel good or bad and think about the solutions.

For example, if you felt bad on a Tuesday, ask yourself why did you feel bad - explore whether this 'bad' meant sad, or angry, or jealous. Once you are successful in labeling your emotions, the next step will be to investigate the cause, why you felt bad, and finally, in the third step, you will think of what you can do to not feel bad again. A sample mood map is given below. You can use this, or make your own.

	Happy	Sad	Angry	Neutral
Monday				
Tuesday				
Wednesday				
Thursday				
Friday				
Saturday				

Sunday				

Exercise 4 - Monitoring Health

I wouldn't call it an exercise, but it is definitely a good practice to have regular health check-ups, including monitoring your blood pressure, weight, sugar levels, and cardiac functions. Any abnormalities noticed must be given proper attention. You may also visit a mental health professional if you are undergoing depression or stress lately, and help them guide you to regain your life and positivity.

Self-Improvement Cheat-Sheet

Conclusion

From the above discussions about emotional intelligence and its impact on the different walks of life, it is clear now that an emotionally intelligent person is one who:

- Can label his/her emotions

- Engage in positive and rational thinking to reach a solution

- Express his/her emotions without hurting others

- Empathizes with people

- Is in control of his/her emotions

Emotional Intelligence is the sum of awareness, balance, expression, and rational thinking. It is an umbrella term that includes aspects of social intelligence, empathy, and communication skills. Unlike general intelligence, E.I. does not grow up to a certain age and stop thereafter. Being emotionally intelligent is a continuous process that we need to work on every day, and the more effort we give in improving it, the more aware do we actually become of ourselves and the world.

The tidbits mentioned in this book along with the self-help exercises will help you in understanding your current level of emotional awareness and which areas you need to focus on improving. So keep your motivation high and aim on making progress each day, as the famous saying goes: *"When emotional intelligence merges with spiritual intelligence, human nature is transformed!"*